Homan
(To Love A Queen)

Homan
(To Love A Queen)

A Touched Body-A Broken Soul-A Healer

T-Rose

In an adult life and an adult situation a child tries to determine what went wrong and why parents aren't meant to be together forever. Young girl becomes an adult too soon and experience the worse in a relationship. How can she bounce back? This is for all the single parents who thought they couldn't make it and all the women in the world who has had to suffer the hardships of love, lust and dependency.

authorHOUSE®

AuthorHouse™
1663 Liberty Drive
Bloomington, IN 47403
www.authorhouse.com
Phone: 1-800-839-8640

First published by AuthorHouse   07/26/2011

ISBN: 978-1-4634-4111-1 (sc)
ISBN: 978-1-4634-4110-4 (ebk)

Library of Congress Control Number: 2011913215

Printed in the United States of America

If Love Was Enough To Hold A Relationship Together Would It?

I know there are many people who experience the pain that comes from love. Love is supposed to be a good thing. I know as well as many other women in this world knows the wrong kind of love can be a very bad thing.

Today was a good day. Tom didn't abuse me in any kind of way. You see today he went to work. Night after night I lay in bed praying Tom would stay out all night and not come home until after I have left for work. It never failed he would come home smelling of liquor and weed. I could hear him call my name. I would just act as if I were sleeping. I knew he wouldn't bother me if I were sleep. I often thought of running away. What good would that do? He would just find me and convince me to come back home. I had to think of my babies and not myself.

I started school in the spring, that is when things got better and a little worse. I met my future husband. He was everything I wanted and everything I needed. I started talking to him on a regular basis. I had even called him on my cell phone one night. Tom was in the kitchen drinking and playing cards with his buddies. I thought I was getting away with a little secret. Little did I know, I had blown my cover. I had said his name and Tom heard it. Things got worse, a whole lot worse.

The weeks followed that had to be the hardest week's I had ever lived. The relationship between Tom and I soon ended. It was not a happy ending. I was harassed by Tom every chance he got. His family was giving me grief, it soon had gotten to the point where I had to get police protection for me. On down the line I gave in to temptation the wrong thing to do. It only made things worse. John always tried to encourage me to work things out with Tom. The more I tried the worse it got.

Tom always blamed me for his misfortunes, knowing all the time it was not my fault. Tom is now history. I am a happier person and I have learned a valuable lesson in love. Love doesn't supposed to hurt. Love is supposed to feel good as a spring day. john and I are together and we are very happy. The wrong kind of love is no good for any relationship. Love is not abuse, it is not mean, it is not spiteful, it is honesty, faithfulness and pure. If you are experiencing the wrong love then it is time to get out of that relationship, it won't save a relationship.

(For all the Toms In the world with a good woman by there sides)-T-Rose

Introduction

When Is Enough, Enough?

This story has two parts. The first is told from my mom's point of view. The second part is told from my point of view (her child). This story is based on facts, although the names have been changed to protect people's privacy. Love has no age limit but it would be a good thing if the maturity levels were up in standards. Tee was a young girl with a maturity level higher than most adults. She never thought love had a age limit. You either loved them or you didn't. Tee also never knew the difference between love, lust and dependency. She would end up learning the biggest lesson in love, life and a relationship before most young people would have had a chance to experience something of this sort. A young lady becomes a woman and learns the hardships of love and the world at an early age. Will this make or break her? Oh well here we go.

The Beginning

It was a nice hot summer day with a breeze, I was 17 and carefree. I was visiting my cousin and his wife (who just happened to be a family friend) when I met Sammy. We were out walking and Sammy and a group of military men were hanging out. I remember telling Susan, "I hope they don't say nothing to us. I hate talking to strangers". Susan was a flirt, married or not she was going to flirt. As always she began to strut so hard I thought her hips would pop out of place. I am sure her strutting got their attention. *Hey good looking*! I tried to act like I didn't hear that remark. After the third time Susan realized I was ignoring this arrogant person, and hit me on the arm saying, "*They talking to you, I am married!*" Now she wanted to act like she was married. Sammy approached us we spoke, as soon as I said hello he asked, "*where you from? You talk different.*" After telling him about the little town I was from we decided to go back to my cousins. Sammy was standing in the middle of the road watching me as I walked away.

The Start of Something

Sammy and I talked the next day. I learned he was 33 years old. He was respectable and handsome. I knew he was into me but at that moment I wasn't thinking on his level. We kept in touched and eventually my cousin and his wife split up and my best friend and my cousin hooked up. The three of us became roommates on the opposite side of town. Sarah was totally different from Susan. She was more outgoing and affectionate. We all ended up being roommates and then Sammy was just a memory. One that kept me smiling.

I really could picture myself with Sammy just didn't know how to go about doing it. My cousin Trey had a friend named Cam. Cam was older, funny, handsome and too much fun. After hanging with Cam for awhile I could see he was somewhat attracted to me. I thought about him a lot as well as Sammy. All I wanted was Sammy, even though it had been months since I'd heard from him. I made up my mind to tell Cam I wanted to use him. I wanted him to teach me how to please an older man. Don't know why I thought age made a difference in the way a lover was treated, but I did. I wrote Cam a letter, didn't know when I would give it to him just knew I would.

> *Cam, don't know how to say this so I will just say it. I want to use you. I want to know what it feels like to be with an older man. I wanna know my limits. I wanna know what makes him tick, laugh and cry. When I say I wanna use you,*

5

I really mean it in a nice way. There will be no strings attached no expectations just living in the moment. I hope you understand what it is I am trying to say.

Love Tee

Later that day Cam stopped by looking for Trey (my cousin). Sarah knew about the letter, she retrieved it from my room and slipped it into his pocket. He never noticed the letter being slipped in his pocket because he was too busy eyeballing me. Sarah said to me "*Let's go out tonight, just us girls. That OK with you?*" I replied, "*Sure why not I need a night out.*" We got dressed, I had on a purple tank dress that hugged every curve I owned. Sarah had on a orange tank dress with flats. We knew we looked good we didn't need anyone to tell us that much. We arrived at Long Horn's at 9pm. We went in and sat at the bar. Neither of us was drinking, we just had to wait to be seated. As soon as we sat at the bar men were coming from every corner! I looked at Sarah and she looked at me, and we each gave each other the nod. The nod was code for no real names and pray for a savior to help us out of this jungle of nothingness. We must have had a dozen marriage proposals, offers for future dates and everything else. An hour had past and the men were still approaching us when I thought there was no escape, Cam walks in. I wanted to shout praises but I knew I had to act as if he wasn't there. As soon as this bad breath brother approached me Cam brushed aside, came towards me and said, "*Baby I am sorry for being late*". Grabbed me by my waist and gently kissed my lips. Can you say SURPRISED! I was stunned but I wasn't the only one so was Sarah. The men started walking away. Peace at last. "*Thanks Cam. Or should I say Baby?*" Cam laughed. Sarah decided to leave. I gave her my car keys, she knew I was in good hands. We were seated at a table in the back. It was nice and smoke free.

"*I got your letter. I understand where you are coming from and I also understand no strings attached. I can handle it if you can.*" Cam was looking straight into my eyes the entire time he was talking to me. It felt so good. "*I can handle it, as long as you understand no strings attached.*" Well we both agreed to the terms and the no string attached relationship had started.

Cam reached across the table grabbed my hand and said "*lesson one. Know you are appreciated, accept appreciation from your man and accepted this kiss to seal our contract.*" Wow it was mind blowing! We ate, we talked and we kissed, then we left. No I didn't sleep with Cam! We hung out for a while that night and many nights after that.

A month had passed and Cam and I was really feeling each other, so I thought. We all ended up at the bowling alley one Saturday evening just hanging and having fun. Then I noticed this girl walking towards Cam. She wasn't bad looking, she wasn't me for sure. She was about 5" 4', maybe 120 pounds and high yellow. Yeah you couldn't tell her, her shit didn't stink her name was Anna and I remember Trey talking about how they had hooked up once before Sarah. Instantly my blood started boiling as soon as I saw her kiss Cam. Sarah grabbed me by the arm and said, "*come on Fido lets take a bathroom break.*" Cam saw me walking away and started to come after me but Trey told him don't, just let me have my time. When we got in the bathroom Sarah said, "*Ain't that some shit! I know you guys don't have that kind of a relationship but hell it is a relationship! I can't believe he did that shit! Why aren't you mad?!?*" I looked at her and said, "*why should I be,? He's only my best friend.*" I couldn't believe I had said that. It was a total lie! Cam was more than a best friend to me. Wow my mind was spinning. I looked at Sarah and said, *"I can't take pain and I am not in the mood for any competition so I am going to just go to my special place. See you later, you know where to find me."* I gave Trey a nod as I walked out. He shook his head, and I gave him this smile as if it was ok. On my way to the car this handsome guy stopped me and said, *"Smiling doesn't cost anything, so why aren't you smiling?"* I looked at him with tears rolling down my face and said, *"It just ain't in me."* He took me by the hand and then he hugged me. I looked into his eyes and said to him, *"Wow your woman must love you."* He looked at me and said, *"I think she does. It was her idea for me to come out here and make sure you were ok we kind of saw what happened."* Oh! Well thank her for me. By the way my name is Tee." "Hello, Tee. My name is Steven and my wife name is Angie." Steven turned and looked towards the door, he looked back at me and said, *"now would be a great time to leave."* Cam was coming towards the door. I looked at Steven and said, *"Good idea, later"*. As soon as Cam came two feet out the door I got in my car and left. I didn't look back.

You could say that bowling alley ordeal was a major setback for me. Cam called me every day and I refused his calls. He would stop by and Sarah would tell him I didn't want to be bothered. I knew our relationship wasn't like Trey's and Sarah's but it was still a relationship and it meant something to me. One day I was out and about just walking on a trail to clear my mind, I noticed I was being followed. I wanted to scream but I knew that was a bad idea. I saw a bench a few feet away from me so I decided to sit and act like I was reading to see if there really was someone following me. As soon as I sat down Cam sat beside me.

Unbelievable! "*Why are you following me?*" "*I just wanted to talk to you*", those was the words that came out of his mouth. "*Make it quick I am trying to read!*" he looked at me as if I had told a corny joke. "*Lesson two, know a man can and will make mistakes. Not all men will apologize when they are wrong. I wasn't trying to hurt you or disrespect you. There will always be other women around but that doesn't mean they are my women.*" I was surprised he was very sincere. His eyes showed his expression. He really looked sad. All I wanted to do was hug him, my pride wouldn't let me. I got up and looked at him and said, "*Lesson learned, although it was painful.*" Cam stood up, looked me in my eyes and said, "*this no strings attached relationship is getting to me. I have been attracted to you for a long time. This is an opportunity no sane man would pass up. I think about you all the time, I hear your voice even when you aren't around, I dream about you and I will gladly give my heart to you, but I know your heart wouldn't be mine*". I couldn't say anything I almost couldn't breathe. I sat back on the bench. My heart was beating fast. I didn't know how to react. I was stunned. After a few minutes of silence I looked at him and said, "*this no string attached relationship doesn't include other people. I will not accept you sleeping with other women. Our no string attached relationship is strictly with us. If and when I decide to be with someone else it's over.*" Cam stood up pulled me close to him, lifted me off the ground and gave me the sweetest hug. he whispered in my ear, "*when this relationship gets stabled I will give you a night to remember*". then he kissed me. Mind blowing!

Cam and I hung out and had fun, no sex just fun. He gave me some great hands on advice about men in general. It was appreciated and taken to heart. Cam came by one day and I was walking around comfortable in a pair old shorts and a tank top. Looking like nothing special. He stopped dead in his tracks. Cam had never seen me with shorts (especially short shorts) on. I was always wearing a pair jeans and a t-shirt or sweat pants and a shirt. "*What is wrong with you? Close your mouth before flies fly in it*". Cam was walking towards me, I started walking backwards. Finally I bumped into the counter. "W*hy are you all up on me!*" He said, "*I can't believe you have been hiding all of this under sweat pants and jeans! Oh my!* All I could do was laugh. He was damn near drooling! "*Cam back up two feet please.*" I said jokingly. "*Why are you here? Trey and Sarah are out in the country for a few days*". Cam had a smile on his face, as he came closer to me and said, "*I didn't come here to see Trey or Sarah. I came here to see you. We need to talk.*" What we need to talk about? Cam why are you still all up on me?" We sat down at the kitchen table sipping on Sprite and talking about nothing. "*Cam what is really on your mind?*" "*Well, I think it is time for lesson 3.*" Lesson 3 what is lesson 3", I asked. He went over to the living room and turned on some jazz. Then he came back to the table and said, "*It is time to see what kind of skills you have in the kitchen!*" I couldn't do anything but laugh.

That night I cooked for Cam, we ate and just enjoyed each other's company. We fell asleep on the couch all cuddled up together. I woke up to someone poking my head, "*What the f**k?!*" It was Trey. "*Good morning sun shines!*", he said. "*What you doing back so soon, what's wrong?*" Cam threw up his hand and went back to sleep. "*Nothing's wrong, I got called in to work.*" "*Where is Sarah*", I asked. "*She stayed in the country she wants you and Cam to come and enjoy the cabin with her.*" An hour later we were on our way to the cabin. We took Cam's car, which probably wasn't the best idea in the world. When we reached the cabin Sarah was coming out the door with her bags in her hand. "*What took you guys so long to get here?*" she asked happily. "*Sarah where are you going?*" Cam and I asked at the same time. "Home, see you guys when you get back on Sunday!" At that moment I realized we had been set up. Dirty dogs. They knew I would not have agreed to come here with Cam alone. I was thirty eight hot! I went into the cabin and damn near passed out when I saw all the roses everywhere. "*What the hell is all of this!*" Just as those words came out my mouth, Cam walked in. "*You like?*" "*Oh man you hate it, damn!*" I turned and looked at Cam and said, "*You did all of this! You planned this behind my back? Why? What were you thinking?*" Cam looked disappointed and sad. "*Tee you don't like it? What's wrong?*" I didn't know if I wanted to laugh or cry. I didn't know how to react to such kindness. I looked at Cam, I was speechless. "*Cam why did you do all of this, why did you go through all the trouble?*" Cam grabbed my hands and looked into my eyes and replied, "*Lesson 4. Let a man cater to you and treat you like a queen. I just wanted you to be happy and carefree. I wanted you to know what it feels like to be truly admired. I wanted you to know how I really feel.*" Tears were rolling down my cheeks I was really touched by his act of kindness. Cam kissed me and I kissed him back, it was filled with passion, it was awesome. We ate dinner by the fireplace picnic style it was sooo nice! We watched movies, we took a midnight stroll and we came back to the cabin and fell asleep in each other's arms.

It was Sunday morning and Cam and I were holding each other close. I looked and Cam and asked, "*Are you going to be able to let go when the time comes?*" He looked at me and replied," *I will deal with that when the time comes.*" We began to hold each other tight. I knew he would have a hard time letting go. Hell I wasn't even sure if I would be able to let go. He had become a part of me and it was a part that I loved. We left the cabin around noon time. We didn't go straight home. Cam wanted me to spend some time with him at his place. Surprising enough his place was breath taking. I asked, *"Do you mind if I take a bath? The heat has me feeling sticky.* Cam looked at me surprised. *"I don't mind. In fact I will run your bath water for you."* Cams place was peaceful, and not at all what I thought it would be. I expected it to be more of a bachelor pad. *"Tee your water is ready. The towels are in the bathroom and there is a robe waiting for you. Is there anything else you need?" Thanks but that is more than enough,"* I said with a smile. Cam showed me to the bathroom. It was nothing I had ever seen before. It was beautiful. An extra large garden tub was in the middle of the floor. It was surrounded by mirrors and candles. I didn't even notice he was burning candles, nor did I notice the rose petals and the music he had playing. *"Well I will leave you to your bath. Is there anything else you will be needing?" "I could use some ice water if you don't mind".* When Cam returned with the ice water I was in the tub covered in bubbles. I was totally relaxed, probably why I didn't noticed Cam was getting into the tub with me. *"Cam what are you doing?" "I thought I would keep you company."* Cam positioned himself behind me so I would be laid back on his chest. *"Don't be getting no bright ass ideas either",* he said with a huge smile on his face. I laughed. He was so much fun. Cam knew what to do and what not to do, in the tub he was a gentlemen. We talked about what men wanted and what they didn't want when it came to women, this was lesson 5 mean what you say and say what you mean. *"Tee are you comfortable being here in the tub with me?" "Yes I am." Are you comfortable with me holding you?" "Yes I am." Why are you asking me these questions?" "Tee I want to give all my love to you to night, are you comfortable with that?"* I turned around and looked him in his eyes and said, *"took you long enough!"* You can guess what happened next. It was amazing!

We arrived back at my place about 10:30 pm with dinner for four. *"Damn what yall do get lost?"* Trey said with this cheesy grin on his face. *"Shut up Trey*! Cam and I said at the same time. Sarah motioned for me to go in the kitchen. Trey and Cam went into the living room and started talking and watching TV. *"girl you are glowing! Are you mad because we didn't tell you about the cabin?* I looked at Sarah and I said, *"I am not mad, I was at first. Then I realized how sweet it was. Thank you!"*

We fixed the plates and we all ate in the living room. Trey and Sarah was surprised when Cam started feeding me. We were so wrapped up in each other that we didn't even noticed they were starring until Cam kissed me and Trey said, *"What the hell is going on?"*

"I knew you couldn't do it, damn! Yall attached." We looked at each other and then them and laughed. It was nice but sometimes even nice doesn't last long.

About two months later Cam and I was just not getting along. There was so much tension and I didn't even know where it was coming from. Of course I got mad told him what I was really feeling and he stormed out. It had been about a week since I heard from him. I was so pitiful. Even Trey saw it. So one day Trey came home and said, *"I need you to ride with me. I can't stand seeing you like this."* Reluctantly I got dressed and did my hair. *Trey said, "don't get mad but I have to blindfold you."* I am thinking to myself damn where we going that is so secretive. I agreed to be blind folded. Finally the car stopped and Trey removed the blindfold. *"Stay here I will be right back."* Wow I knew where we were. We were in the same spot where I met Sammy. What I didn't know was why we were here. About five minutes later Trey came out and said "don't be mad." I looked up and there was Sammy. I was almost in tears. I haven't heard from him in months. I couldn't do anything but hug him and it felt so good. He held me tight. He was like, "I thought I never would see you again. I had no idea where you had moved to. It got so bad that I went to Trey while he was at work and asked if he knew where you were. "Happy belated birthday!" Then he gave me a soft kiss. Trey was standing by the car on the phone with Sarah crying, too funny. We said our goodbyes and exchanged numbers. I could not believe Trey took me to see Sammy. I was all smiles.

Sarah and I was cleaning and it had been a week since I saw Sammy. I thought about him every day and I thought about Cam too. I showered, put on a white body shirt and a pair of shorts. I was laying across my bed when Sarah knocked on the door and told me I had company. I couldn't even imagine who would be coming to see me. To my surprise it was Sammy. Looking good as ever in his uniform. I spoke and then he hugged me. Then he took a step back and said "*Damn, you been hiding all that!*" I was blushing. He pulled me close to him and just looked at me. We walked in the yard. We talked for a while and then he had to leave. He was on his lunch break. Cam pulled up. My eyes got big. Sammy said, "*is that your boyfriend you always talking about?*" I said, "A friend." Sammy said bye and left before Cam got out his car. Sammy was mad and I could tell. Sammy saw Cam as my boyfriend because that is what I wanted him to believe. Cam knew who Sammy really was and he looked even madder than Sammy. "*Was that the punk in the uniform?*" he asked with plenty of attitude. I couldn't do nothing but smile. Cam was jealous. I was tickled. I turned to go into the house and Cam grabbed me by the arm and pulled me close to him. Looked me in my eyes and said, "*I am not letting you go that easily.*" I didn't know if I should be flattered or scared. I looked at Cam and said, "*your grip is a little too tight let go, now!*" Cam apologized and pulled me into his arms. My head was spinning. I didn't even know which way I was going and how to get there. This wasn't good at all. What Cam and I had felt so damn good, but was it true? I was torn between the two. This was not going to be a good situation in the end.

Cam and I was watching TV when the phone rang. I answered it and it was Sammy. "*I need to see you can I stop by tomorrow?*" "*Yes tomorrow will be a good day to show some paintings I will meet you at 5pm. See you then.*" Sammy knew this was code for, I am not alone. Cam didn't think nothing of the phone call. He was going to be working the next three days. That is why we were hanging out tonight. Cam turned off the TV and turned on the music. We must have talked until 3 am. Cam left at 3:30. He gave me a kiss and hugged me tight. I didn't want to let him go. We kissed for a long time then he said "*I have to go get ready for work. I love you Tee.*" What? He loved me! I could not believe I heard those words come from his mouth. Oh my!

I was getting out the shower when I heard a knock on the door. Who the world is at the door this time of morning. It was 6am. I grabbed a towel and went to the door. It was Sammy. He wasn't in uniform either. "*What are you doing here so early?*" I forgot I was standing with a towel around me and water still dripping from my body. "*Sammy, what's wrong?*" He was just standing there with his mouth open. ".*Come in.*" I closed the door behind me as I pushed Sammy into the living room. Finally he said, "*I couldn't sleep.*" "*Well I have some phone calls to make. You are welcomed to stay and eat breakfast with me.*" I dried off and slipped on a t-shirt and underwear. I made my phone calls to my clients and then I cooked breakfast for the two of us. Sammy told me how he felt about me. I was surprised. We decided to be friends and see what happens. Sammy gave me a hug and a kiss and he left. Sammy and I spent a lot of time together. Cam and I spent a lot of time together as well. We were renovating the house and I decided to visit my sister until the work was finished. I drove to my sister house with Sammy. We stayed for a while and chilled with her and the family. I drove Sammy back home. We had a good time together. I gave him a hug and left. I was at my sister's for three weeks and every other day Sammy came to see me. Cam came every day. The funny thing is they barely missed each other when they came to see me. I knew this was getting to be a bit too much for me. Sammy and I wasn't intimate or anything but there were feelings. Cam and I on the other hand was a different story.

Sammy

Eventually Cam and I was done and it was me and Sammy. Sammy and I became closer. He was sweet, he was attentive and he was a true man. Sammy and I had a relationship different from mine's and Cam's. I missed Cam but it was what it was. I decided to move out on my own, just because it was the right thing to do. Trey and Sarah wasn't pleased with my decision at all. I gave them a house key, and left. Trey was smiling. He didn't expect to have a key to my house.

Sammy had roommates, I really didn't like being at his house because one of the roommates were a true bitch. I was at Sammy's one day when his roommate's wife had her cousin over. I was on the phone talking to Sarah when I heard her ask, "*How old is your girl friend?*" He replied, "she's 18". Then I heard her yell out, "You are a CM (child molester)! Sarah heard it as well. I got my keys, I told Sarah I would see her in a few minutes, and I hung up the phone. I went into the living room where Sammy was. I walked up to the cousin and I asked, "how old are you?" She replied, "20". I looked her in the eyes and said, "*Damn, with the way you act I thought you were 10!*". It was on. The bitch swung on me and missed. I leaped and knocked her ass on the floor laid a blow straight to the nose. Stood over her and said, "*Don't mistake a real woman for a child and I don't date child molesters!*" Sammy didn't know what the hell to think. I kissed him and I left. I was mad as hell. When I met Sarah at the mall, my hand was swollen. She said, "*You hit that bitch huh?*" I looked at her with a smile and said, "*Laid*

17

her ass out !" We laughed. I heard someone say, "*What's up beautiful!*" It was Cam. I turned around and looked at him. He looked at me and said, "*What got you mad?*" He noticed my hand. "*You been fighting!*" "*It was hardly a fight*", I said. "*Well somebody got knocked the hell out! Your hand is swollen badly. That punk tried to hit you?* Cam was serious and bout to catch a case. "*Cam it is nothing for you to worry about. No it wasn't Sammy it was his roommate's cousin. She said something I didn't like.*" Cam had this worried look in his eyes as well as Sarah. The three of us shopped and we ate lunch. Cam mostly starred at me. I could tell he wanted to touch me. Sarah went to Penny's and we sat in the food court and talked. Cam moved over beside me and asked, "*you want to talk about it?*" I had tears in my eyes. I didn't want to look at him. He put my face in his hands and looked into my eyes and said, "*I don't like seeing you hurt! I don't like seeing you with him! I don't like being without you!*" My heart was crying, I was sobbing. Cam pulled me close to him and held me. I couldn't even talk, I just cried.

Two weeks later I was painting my kitchen and Sammy stopped by. He was in uniform. "*I haven't seen you in two weeks. You didn't stop by. You didn't return my calls. I was worried. What's wrong?*" I looked at him, put my paint brush down and said, "*no need to worry I can handle myself!*" "*Oh so you are mad at me, why?*" I could not believe he was standing here acting like his ass didn't know why I was mad! "*To enlighten you on the situation, you could have defended yourself! Those were harsh words and I didn't appreciate it. Did you think it was cute? Hell I didn't !It pissed me off!*" He shook his head. "*So you had to break her nose for what she said?*" I could not believe this shit. He was defending her! "*Hell yea I had to break her damn nose! I didn't like the words that came out of her mouth! Maybe next time she will think before she opens her mouth! I bow down to no bitch and that includes you!"* Sammy was clearly stunned. He couldn't even say nothing. "*I tell you what Sammy you take your ass and get the hell out of my house! I want a man that can defend himself, a man with a fucking backbone!*" Sammy started walking towards me with this look in his eyes. I didn't know what was in his brain. I was already in defense mode. He grabbed my arms and pulled me close to him and said to me, "*Don't ever take me for a weak ass man! My backbone is mighty strong and one day you will experience what my backbone can do for you!* He kissed me. He apologized to me. He kissed me again. He looked me in my eyes and asked, "*did you have to break her nose?*" All I could do was laugh.

Sammy and I moved in together (well he moved in with me). It was nice. Nice don't last for long. My cousins had stopped by one day and we were catching up. Sammy was out and about. We heard a knock at the door my cousin answered it. It was a heavy set woman looking for Sammy. My cousin told her he was out and asked who should she say was looking for him. Her name was Monique, she was a school teacher and she had it bad for Sammy. My cousins went into defense mode. Monique left. "That bitch thought she was the stuff! An hour later Sammy walked in. He spoke to everybody and gave them a hug. My cousin Trish said, "*Sammy, Monique stopped by. She wasn't so thrilled to see a house full of women. She got it bad for you. Something you want to tell us about?* Sammy looked around the room and said, "*there is nothing to tell.*" We all said at the same time, "*Bullshit!*" Sammy looked at us and laughed. "*Yall crazy!* He finally told us the story of a wanna be stalker. My cousins stayed another hour and then they left.

Sammy instantly went into beast mode after they left. We argued for hours. Finally I told him to "*get the hell out of my house"*. We both left the house at the same time. I didn't care where he went and if he came back I was tired of the bullshit. When I was sure I wasn't been followed I called Sarah. Her and Trey was Out for the night, but she said I could lay low at their place and the key was in the same spot it always in, under the flower pot. I got to Sarah and Trey's house about 20 minutes after I hung up with Sarah. It was dark there were no lights left on. I locked my car and carefully made my way to the porch. As I walked up the stairs I heard a voice ask, *"Where you going this time of night?"* It was Cam. *"Cam you idiot you trying to give me a heart attack?! Damn!"* Cam was laughing. He walked towards me and grabbed my hands and guided me up the steps. We sat on the porch with candles and talked. *"Cam what are you doing here?"*

He was holding my hands. He said, *"Waiting for you. Sarah said you may need a shoulder to lay on. Is that true?"* I didn't know what to think. Cam is always there when I need someone to just be a friend, Amazing. *"yes it is true, I do need a friend. I don't want to talk about my problems. I just need to be held."* Cam stood up and grabbed my hands. I stood up and we went into the house. Cam was truly more than a friend but he wouldn't cross that line for anything in the world and that is what I admired the most about him. We watched TV until we fell asleep. I left early the next morning. I left Cam still asleep. I went home and got in the shower. As I was getting out the shower Sammy was standing in front of me. He had just came in. I screamed. *"What the hell are you doing? Damn!"* Sammy was laughing. *"I didn't mean to scare you. I was going to knock on the shower door but you opened it. Nice view!"* Damn I was standing there naked as a jay bird. I pushed him out the way and got my robe and put it on. *"Can we talk Tee?"* *"There is nothing for us to talk about."* Just then it dawned on me. Sammy and I had been together for eight months and not once had we had sex. I think that was my choice but I was pretty sure that was the subject for the day. *"Tee I love you! I want to give you the world! I want you to be the mother of my kids!"* Wow I was stunned. Sammy walked towards me. He pulled me close, looked into my eyes and said, *"I love you so damn much, it hurts!"* My heart was truly touched. he picked me up into his arms and kissed me. He kissed me all over. It was like a dream when we made loved. We held each other afterwards, talked and made love some more.

I woke up and I was feeling different. I felt sick or something. It wasn't bad but it wasn't good either. I had just had my birth control shot two days ago. I never felt like this. I shook it off and went on about my day. It had been a few weeks since I woke up feeling sick. Seems like it had gotten worse. Everything I tried to eat bothered me in some kind of way. I just thought I had a bug or something. Finally I noticed a lump under my left arm. It was painful, so I told Sammy about it. I ended up at the ER. Feeling like uhh! The doctor came in they took blood and they ran numerous tests just to be on the safe side. An hour later the doctor came in and he says, *"Ms Jones you are six weeks. The baby is fine and so are you."* I was in shock. I was thrilled. I was scared. I was scared of Sammy's reaction. I was just plan scared. I got dressed after the nurse gave me my paper work and I went to the check out desk and left. Sammy kept looking at me strangely. Finally he asked, *"Are you going to tell me what is wrong?"* I gave him the papers and then I went into the living room. He stormed in the living room, picked me up off the couch and kissed me. He was overly excited and I was in tears. My hormones were off the chart. Sammy pampered me. Everything I needed Sammy made sure I had it. He took a trip to Denver. I was alone I called my brother to stay with me for a week. He was in and out but that was better than being by myself. Sarah and Trey came by a few times. I hadn't heard from Cam in months. I didn't dare to ask about him although I really wanted to. Time went on and I got bigger. My mom came and stayed with me for a while. Even before she came she would always meet me at my doctor appointments. We went to my appointment and I was actually due that day. They sent me home because I wasn't having contractions and the baby hadn't dilated. Two days later I went back for my appointment, my mom was with me. My blood pressure was sky high. They rolled me to labor and delivery, induced my labor and waited. Mom Called Sammy. I didn't want family there it was already too stressful for me. The nurse came in and she said Ms Jones you have a phone call. I looked at mom, she looked at me. no one knew I was here other than Sammy and he had just left. "*Hello*", I said really low. On the other end there was a woman fussing at me. "*You thought we wouldn't find you? You ain't having that baby without us!*" then the phone was hung up. My mom looked at me and I looked at her and I said, "*they found me!*" We laughed so hard. As the night progressed I was in so much pain it was time for my epidural and I was scared. I hated needles especially long needles that had to go into your back. I had to have this done 5 times. No this wasn't normal at all. The first time I moved, the second time the line slipped out, third time the line had a bubble in it that blocked the medicine, the fourth time something happened I don't know what and the fifth time it was a success. Through all five of them I was getting some of the medicine. I was on cloud 99 by the time they finished with me. I was so out of it that I really can't remember everything, only what family tells me.

I had my aunts, cousins, sister, mom and friends there just didn't know it. I also never knew the danger I was in. I remember everyone coming in the room and saying, "*you will be alright we will get through this together, We will see you in a few minutes. you will be alright.*" I was so exhausted and out of it. The baby weighed 7 pounds and 2 ounces. She was beautiful and looked just like her Dad. He was so happy. I do remember him kissing me and saying, "*I love you.*" Anything after that was a blur. From the start my pregnancy was a high risk pregnancy and dangerous. I am just glad everything was good with us.

I went home before the baby. I really didn't want to leave her. She stayed an extra two days. Although I was supposed to be on bed rest I went to see my baby up until the day I brung her home. Sammy was the proud father, as soon as she came home he took her for a walk. All the neighbors just adored her.

Sienna was 6 months when we moved to a bigger house, one with a large yard for her to play in. Sammy worked and I stayed home with the baby. Things seemed to be good. Then I started noticing that Sammy was hardly home with us. He was either working or out with his friends but he never hardly spent quality time with his family. Sienna and I would go visit Sarah and Trey and other family members, but Sammy was never with us. This became a pattern. Finally one night when Sammy came home I approached him and asked him, "*Is it hard for you to spend time with us?*" He tried to act like I was over reacting. I told him, "*When you get back from work we will be gone*". That is what I meant. When he got home the next day we were in Atlanta with relatives for 3 weeks. He called and called and each time he called I made sure we were out and about. Finally we were getting ready to go and eat when my aunt gave the phone to me. It was Sammy. "*how are you doing? I called but you were out. Are you coming back home soon I miss you and the baby.*" I could tell he was in tears because his voice was shaking. "*We will be home in a day or two.*" I said. I put Sienna on the phone she was just babbling, but Sammy was happy to hear that.

We returned home two days after I had talked to Sammy. He wasn't there when we arrived. I gave Sienna a bath feed her and put her to sleep. As I was walking out of her room Sammy walked towards me. He looked into my eyes and with tears rolling down his face he said, "*Please don't leave like that again. I love you and I love my child. I didn't mean to hurt you in any way*". We hugged each other and held each other tight. It wasn't long after we returned Sammy was doing the same shit. I spent most of my time with friends and family. Finally it dawned on me I was nothing more than a trophy for him. Whenever he had a function to go to and wanted to look as if he was a true family man then we would spend time together being a family just to impress friends. We were at a wedding, I had on this little black dress. I was looking the part for sure. The ushers were arguing over who would walk me to my seat. Oh Sammy was grinning from ear to ear. As long as his friends were drooling over his trophy that gave him big status. They could look and drool all day long but never could they talk to me or touch me. I greeted everyone I saw with a pleasant smile and a hello. Truth be told I was totally out of place, at least that is how I felt. I was 20 in a crowd with mostly 30+ adults. Another wedding I wore this pant suit and it was the same reaction from his friends. Yep I was indeed his trophy. Not all of his friends treated me like a trophy some were kind of cool. I hardly went with him to hang out with his friends. I can honestly say Sienna has spent more time with his friends and their wives than I have. He wanted to make it seem as if we were a very happy family. Truth be told I wasn't happy.

Eventually one of Sammy's skeletons was revealed. He had a habit one that I truly detested. Yep he was doing drugs. What it was he was doing I wasn't sure. All I know is he would just blow up at me at the drop of a dime. One day he stormed into the bedroom got in my face and started lashing out at me. That was the first time he told me,he wasn't in love with me, he was in love with his child. His eyes were dangerous his voice was fierce and I was scared. I was pinned in a corner he was calling me everything but a child of God, he was telling me how useless I was and that I would never be nothing more than a piece of ass. He stormed out of the house and I was in that corner shocked and crying. I felt like nothing. Just worthless. This kind of outburst happened many times after, and every time it got worse. I realized that I was in an abusive relationship. It wasn't physical but abuse of any kind is abuse. I kept telling myself it was me, in my heart I knew it wasn't me.

I treated Sammy with respect no matter how he treated me. It was his birthday of course he was out the entire day but when he got home he had a nice dinner waiting for him and our bedroom was filled with balloons, the floor was covered. I was asleep wearing a red silk teddy with hearts and on the end of the bed were a pair of red silk boxers with hearts. I was surrounded by balloons. To my surprised he acted like the Sammy I was used to the nice one. He showered he put the boxers on and we made love for hours. It was unbelievable. I knew he enjoyed it because days after he was still thanking me for his birthday present. Sex wasn't a problem in our relationship. The problem was Sammy not being home or spending time with us.

One day some of my girlfriends were over and we were hanging out and doing hair. We were eating Bar-B-Que Fritos and having fun. I noticed I was feeling light headed but I never mentioned it to anyone. After they had left I was watching TV when Sammy came home from work. He gave me a kiss and asked were Sienna was. I told him she was playing with Kat next door. He looked at me and asked, *"Are you alright? You look pale"* I told him I think I might have gotten too hot because I felt really hot. Sammy went into the bedroom to take a shower, I sat back in the chair. As soon as my behind touched the chair I jumped straight up and ran for the guest bathroom. I threw up all the Bar-B-Que Fritos I had eaten earlier. Some splashed on the floor the mop was in my bedroom. I went to my bedroom to get the bleach and the mop out of our bathroom. Sammy asked, *"What are you doing with the mop? You just mopped everything yesterday."* I looked at him and I said, *"I am mopping the other bathroom, I threw up and some got on the floor."* He looked at me and said, *"Damn you pregnant!"* I was shocked. Honestly I was thinking more on the line of a bug or something. Later that day I felt better didn't have much of an appetite but I felt better. I did notice I had an unbearable pain in my right side. I just ignored it for a while and just did what I normally did.

Sienna had turned four and just like any of her other birthdays and her parties, Sammy wasn't around for long. He would buy loads of presents and leave before the party started. I sometimes wondered how I endured this bullshit daily. There were 40+ people at this party. We had two huge cakes, each could feed 80 people. We had family, friends and neighbors there but no Sammy. It was awesome. Sienna enjoyed herself. My best friend (Kelly)was there, as well as her mom. Her mom pulled me to the side and she said to me, "*you are three weeks pregnant*". I was stunned so stunned that I laughed. I didn't know what to think. I knew she had the gift to foretell some things but this was scary. Sure enough she was right. I was hurting and sick as hell. I went next door to Nichole's only to find her in the bed and she said she was sick. She woke up that way and so did I. My side was hurting and I couldn't hardly stand. Two days later after enduring all the pain I could Kelly drove me to the ER. She went to the grocery store while I was at the ER. The doctor ran some tests did a serious of x-rays and came back into the room thirty minutes later and said, "*I have some good news and some bad news.* "My heart was racing. I couldn't imagine what it was he was going to tell me. I looked at him, took a deep breath and said, "*Give me the bad news first.*" He looked at the charts and said, "*You are very dehydrated and you have a golf ball size cyst on your right ovary.*" What is the good news?" You are pregnant!" I honestly in any other life, any other given time I would be running over with joy At this moment I was crying. I wasn't crying because I didn't want another child. I was crying because Sammy didn't want any more children. I didn't have a clue as to when I would tell him. As I was getting ready my cell phone wrung. It was my friend Nichole. I told her the news and I told her not to mention it to Sammy. Kelly was in the waiting room when I walked in t here. "*Chick you look terrible and you have been crying. What's wrong?*" We walked to the car in silence. We were almost to my house when I told Kelly about the cyst and the baby. I should have waited because we were almost in a ditch. We had to pull over. She was too excited about the baby. I was crying so hard she didn't know what to think. I told her why I was crying and she was shocked. I knew she would have my back no matter what. An hour after I got home Sammy came storming in the house mad as hell. He grabbed my arm and shoved me into the room. "*When the hell was you going to tell me? When the damn baby got here? You can't have this child! Get rid of it! I am too damn old for another child! I can't play with that child walking on a got damn cane! What the fuck were you thinking? How dumb could you be!*" This went on until I grabbed my keys and Sienna and got the hell out of there. I ended up at Kelly's. "*He called here looking for you. I told him you haven't called and you haven't been here. Tee don't let him make that decision for you. I know you don't believe in abortions. Don't let him make you feel like you are nothing. Don't give him that!*" *We can raise this child with or without him. This is my Godchild, this child will be just fine.*" I didn't sleep good that night. Sammy blew up my cell phone. Finally I turned it off. Those words echoed in my head over and over and over again. Those words sliced my heart and my soul.

I was five months and Sammy was distant. He always wanted to hold me and make love to me. That wasn't enough. Sienna was so happy. She would tell everybody, "*We gonna have a baby. It will be my baby and my mom's.* I was very ill. Food made me sick just to smell it. Jolly ranchers and plain Cheerios were my best friend. Sienna would always crawl next to me no matter where I was sitting and put her mouth close to my belly and say, "*Hey my little baby! Kick if you can hear me.*" Sure enough the baby would kick. Even if Sienna wasn't talking to the baby it would kick whenever she was around. One thing for sure they had a bond and that meant the world to me.

Sade is born

I was sleeping but I was in pain. I woke up and got my watch. I figured it could be contractions but I wasn't sure. I put three pillows behind me and continued to sleep sitting up. The pain was like 25 minutes apart. Finally I woke up with this urge to go to the bathroom. My pain was about every 6 minutes. I woke Sammy up and told him it was time. This was truly my first time experiencing true labor pains. Sammy dressed Sienna and we went to the ER. It had to be the worst ride. Sammy must have hit every pot hole in the road not to mention train tracks. Of course he couldn't stay with Sienna. He went back home and called my friend Bertha. Bertha had already said she wanted to be there from start to finish. It was about 11am when Bertha arrived. She arrived just in time, my contractions were off the chain. I had an epidural earlier, the only way I knew I was having a contraction (besides that machine recording them) was when I got this tight squeezing feeling in my upper left thigh. Bertha was off the chain! She was tripping. She had to go take a smoke break. She came back and said, "*Let's get this show on the road. We want a Jerry Springer baby!*" Sade was born two minutes after Jerry Springer came on. She looked just like her sister. Bertha went home to change and to get her family so they could come see me and the baby. Their visit was nice. Later that night I was having terrible pain in my neck. When the nurse came in to check my blood pressure she asked, "*Are you in pain? Your blood pressure has elevated*". All I could do was nod, I could barely move my neck. The doctor came in, he examined me and even did an x-ray. Finally he said, "*It appears that when we gave you your epidural air was in the line and that is why you are experiencing some pain. We will give you a high dosage of Ibuprofen and a lot of caffeine. So throughout the night I need you to drink everything the nurse put on your tray. You should feel a bit better by morning.*" Well I didn't sleep that night. The next morning the nurse had brung Sade in the room. She was such a good baby and very alert. After feeding and drying her I laid her down to take a nap. When she was sleep I went to the bathroom to freshen up. When I came out of the bathroom I heard voices and I heard Sade making little baby noises. It was Kelly and her nieces. Kelly was crying. "*Tee she is so precious!*" She noticed the IV, "*what's up with the extra meds?*" I told her about my neck. "*So that is why your hair isn't done huh?*" Kelly had jokes. She put Sade down pulled out her hair bag and braided my hair. Kelly was dating my brother who decided to go get a pale version of a woman without her knowledge so when she found out it was hell. My brother had talked to her and not once mentioned I was in the hospital. Men can be stupid sometimes. I had a lot of visitors but not one of them was Sammy. When he finally came to the hospital my friend Jan was visiting me and she had the baby. Jan was seven months pregnant and always hungry. As a matter of fact she was eating my lunch! Too funny. Of course as soon as he sees her he acting the part. He spoke, gave me a kiss and reached for the baby. "*She looks just like Sienna*! he was excited, but not excited enough to sign her birth certificate. His excuse was he was in a hurry he was on his way to court. Sure he was, damn liar! A few days later we were released from the hospital, Bertha picked us up. The house was spotless when I got home but no Sammy, he was at work. Sienna was at school. I laid Sade in the middle of my bed. Bertha was getting her bath water ready for her first bath. Bertha was so excited. I pinned a bunch of pretty pink ribbons on the door. So when my neighbor went to pick the kids up from the bus stop they all were there looking at the baby. They could not believe she was so small. Sienna was so happy. She washed her hands, changed her clothes and climbed on my bed and gave Sade a kiss. Yep I was pretty sure she knew who Sienna was because she was smiling. Too cute. the funny thing was there were three newborns in our family, my sister's baby was born six days before mines and Kelly's baby was born about two months before mine's. Kelly and I was going through some things, but that is another story for another day.

I was laying in the bed with Sade when Sammy came home. Sienna was in his arms just talking away about the baby and me being in pain. *"Tee, are you ok?"* I am guessing the tears gave me a way. He put Sienna down, got two very hot towels and put them on my neck. he kissed me and said, *"I hope you feel better soon. The towels should help".* Sade was woke. She was just looking around. Sammy took Sade and Sienna into the living room with him so I could get some rest. Sienna was very attentive when it came to Sade. She stayed on the couch with her whenever Sammy came to check on me. She always wanted to help with the diaper change. The only thing she couldn't help with was the feeding, she was strictly breast fed.

Sammy wasn't as distance any more. I noticed when Sade got to be a few months older she didn't care for Sammy. No matter who had her she was a good baby until her father would hold her she would cry. He said she was spoiled. She only cried with him. Sammy and I wasn't close anymore. I tried to act like everything was all right but it wasn't and it hadn't been in a while.

The Struggle

Sammy was retired from the Navy. He found another job. I guess it wasn't what he wanted because pretty soon he was talking about going to Denver and finding work and returning to Texas to get us when he had found work. The day came when he left for Denver. He held me so tight, he kissed me so long. He looked into my eyes and said, "*I will be home every weekend. Distance only makes the heart grows fonder. I love you guys.*" He called every night. We would talk for hours. In the beginning he even came home every weekend. Then it was every other week end. Then every two weeks and finally he stopped. The phone calls became less. I knew something wasn't right the last time he came home and that something would not let me make love to him although he wanted to. It was official Sammy would not be coming back. He had a new girlfriend and wanted very little to do with us. I was devastated. My world had been shattered. Seven years I gave to this man just for him to walk away and never look back. Friends tried to comfort me, family tried to down me and strangers would be the one to help me and my children. I had never know pain in this form in my life! I never knew humiliation until now! I felt as though I had lost everything. If it had not been for my kids I would have given up. Sammy wouldn't send money to help with the bills. I was ill and didn't even know it. Whenever I was around family I could hear them whispering about me. They would say, "*She is just pitiful. She knew he wasn't no good when she got with him. She just stupid. Ain't no need for her to ask us for nothing. She got herself into this mess she got to deal with it. Is she sick she so small? He probably gave her something and left her ass to deal with it. She knew she didn't need no more children when she got pregnant with the second one. Damn shame walking around her looking like death cause some man don't want her ass no more. Stupid ass!"* Believe me it was worse than that. Eventually I just stopped visiting family. I pretty much knew when I wasn't wanted. It was hard and there were days where I didn't think I was going to make it. Not being able to provide for my kids was the worse feeling.

Holidays were the worst time for us. Finally I sat Sienna down and told her we would not have Christmas anymore because we could not afford it. She was very understanding. She hugged me and said, *"Mommy don't cry, we still love you. We don't have to do Christmas."* Family made sure they had something during the holidays. I didn't care I was done with holidays. Sienna's attitude started to change. She was fighting at school. Sammy had affected her in so many ways and he really didn't give a damn. It was hard for Sienna because she was a daddy's girl. Yet she felt the need to be strong for me. All I can say is when it rain it pours. If this was a test from Heavenly Father it was one I wasn't sure I could pass.

It wasn't long before the struggle really began. We had no electricity and then no water. I had to go to different churches asking for help. Felt more like begging for handouts. they were really nice and the first time they did pay the electric bill. The school had rezoned so Sienna had to go to a different school one that was a little farther away. She did well at his school. We were without electricity and water for months. If it wasn't for our neighbors I don't know what we would have done. I had friends of my neighbor coming by the house giving us money and helping any way they could. One guy came to the house and he said to me, "*no disrespect intended but, I thought you being young and all you would have gone to the extreme for your kids and start doing tricks.*" That was a mouthful. I didn't know how to take that. He looked at me and said, "*I didn't mean you should, guess I am just proud to see a young single mom doing right by her kids even if she is struggling. Just know you will get through this and in the end you will be a better person. No matter how hard it gets don't ever give up!*" He then gave me this box and said, "*It ain't much but it is all I got that is worth something and I would rather give it to someone who needs it than hold on to it and do nothing.*" After he left I opened the box. It was filled with baseball, football, and basketball cards. Most of them were rookie cards dating back to the early 60's. A completed stranger had given me such a heartfelt gift, some good advice and a blessing. I was truly touched. Kelly was my crutch throughout this struggle. She was there from beginning to end.

I vowed to never open my heart up and love again. I put shackles and chains around my heart so no one could ever hurt me again. I vowed to never ever let my kids suffer at the hands of a man ever again. I might have dated one guy after Sammy and it wasn't nothing more than a friendship. Al was good to talk to but useless in other things. We hung but eventually I told him I needed some me time and he deserved someone who would adore him I was just going through the motions and probably could not love a man ever again.

The one lesson I did learn was when you are down never ever count on family. My family damn near cost me my kids. They said I was an unfit parent that knew little about parenting. I wasn't in tune with God. I was nothing more than a backslider who was getting exactly what she deserved. Family. You got to love them.

Eventually the kids and I had to go stay at this transitional home. A home for women with drug problems and other issues. I could not believe I was in a place like this. I felt like I had sunken lower than low. I had to do this for months because my family called family and children services on me. I could not for the life of me figure out why they hated me so much. I had done nothing wrong. All I did was try to provide for me and my children the best way I could without doing anything stupid or illegal. It was hell. The owner was a fake pastor who swore she was some kind of prophet or something. I hated church with a passion. I guess you could say it was the people that I hated the most. The ones who judged a person and don't know what that person is going through. I found a church (before coming here) that I could find peace in and now I wasn't even able to go. What the hell! I was beyond depressed. Most of my time was spent crying and asking God why was I being punished. My daily and nightly prayers were covered in many tears. Something inside would not let me quit. I don't know where the drive to keep going came from but it was there. I wanted better for my kids and I was going to turn this situation around. We stayed in that awful place for three months. Then a friend bailed us out. We stayed at her place for two weeks and then returned to our home. Our neighbors embraced us with tears. They had came up with some funds to have our electricity and water turned back on while we were gone. My heart was over joyed. They wanted nothing in return just to see me and the kids make it. I never knew there was such a kindness in the world until that day. I always thanked them for their kindness. Blessing go up and results come down.

Finally I got this offer from a parent and a friend (Kim). She needed a house cleaner and a baby sitter. Live in house keeper and babysitter. An offer I couldn't refuse. Seeing how Sammy had stopped paying on the house and completely threw us away, I took her up on that offer. When I saw the house I wanted to run! It was more than a mess it looked like a land field. I had my work cut out for me. Let's just say six hours later it looked like a brand new house. This was definitely a blessing with in a blessing.

Better Days

Things were looking up. I had money in my pockets and a roof over our head. What I didn't know was in the coming months Heavenly Father would send me one of his angels. I pretty much had given up on love and dating. My days were spent with my kids and friends. I felt so much better. One day Kim and I was talking and she said her brother would be coming into town and she wanted him to meet me. I was hesitant at first but then I said ok what could be so bad about it. He was nice and not like the rest of the family at all. I was surprised. I was drawn to him but I didn't want anyone to notice that. He was sweet, intelligent, my age and handsome. First thing came to my mind was, "*He will see me and keep going.*" I wasn't ready for love but I could use a distraction. Heavenly Father had something different in mind. I thought me having kids would scare him off. I was wrong. I was getting ready to start working again. Which means I would be moving out. Yep things were looking up. Stefan was a breath of fresh air. We took things slow and day by day. Sienna had a hard time adjusting at first but then she came around. Sade was instantly drawn to him. There were many nights we tried to go out and Sade ended up with us. Stefan didn't seem to mind. We would spend hours just talking to each other. It felt different. It felt honest. It felt a lot like something I had only experienced once before. It dawned on me, I loved Sammy but I wasn't in love with him. That was the difference I was falling in love!

The more we spent time with each other the more the shackles and the chains were released from my heart.

37

He was reassuring and attentive. He was the man who would restore my heart. He was my strength and my new beginning. Stefan was with us when the time came for us to move. He was such a big help. One day while getting our belongings from the house some of my neighbors came by to say good bye and to wish us luck. Stefan was playing basketball with the kids. Charlie my neighbor looked at me and then at the other neighbor Glenda and then his wife Shon. Charlie had this big grin on his face. "*Oh Tee got a boy friend!* I could only blush. "*Be quiet Charlie*! I said jokingly. Glenda said, "*Damn that's alright yall, hell yea our girl is happy*! All I could do was laugh when all of them gave me a hug. I would miss them. They were there even when family turned their backs on me and my kids.

New Job & New Home

It was moving time. I have to say the new place wasn't what I was used to but it came with the job and it could be improved. Sure enough after I sprayed and disinfected the place it was ok. Stefan was such a huge help. Weeks had passed and it really started to feel like home. Stefan and I would talk every night and sometimes during the day for hours at a time. He spent a lot of time with the girls and I. The men in the apartment complex was always saying, *"Stefan is one lucky ass man. If I had what he had I would keep it under lock and key!"* Little did they know I was the lucky one. Stefan was always understanding and we didn't argue we had debates-no screaming was aloud just talking. This was hard for me in the beginning, only because in past relationships I just ignored the man while he screamed at the top of his lungs. It was nice not being yelled at. Everybody in the apartment complex knew who I was as well as my kids. The Owners were kind and down to earth. One was actually a friend(James). He came when he heard what Sammy had done(left us with nothing) and offered me a job. He said it wasn't much but it would help support me and my kids. To be honest I hadn't know kindness on this level existed in the world. Sometimes the human race gets so wrapped up into material things that they just don't see the need to be kind to others.

The new job kept me busy, but I always had time for my kids and Stefan and that was the important part. Stefan stayed with us during his vacation it was nice. He would cook me lunch and watch Sade and get Sienna off the bus.

There were times when I hated to see him leave it would break my heart. The first time I felt like this I knew I had fallen in love. To experience being in love again, for me was such a joy. Stefan was the second guy that I had ever been in love with. The first is just a blur, because I wanted it that way. Threw him away and forgot about his very existence. Kelly and I still talked on a daily basis. Kim came by every other day her and the kids.

Relocating to the City

I had been at this job for a few months not quite a year, when Stefan asked, if the kids and I would move in with him. I was speechless. I knew I didn't need time to think about this, I said yes right then. Someone had been found to replace me. James wasn't happy that I was leaving but he understood. I sold over half of my things, we didn't need two of everything. Finally it was moving day, the truck was loaded and everybody was saying their good byes. The girls and I were in the car, we had one final stop to make, my moms. She didn't want us to leave but at the same time she knew we were happy.

The first week was so hard for me. I was totally homesick. It was unbelievable. I was an emotional wreck. Stefan tried to comfort me and he said it would get better and it did, eventually. Sienna was in school and Sade was home with me. We would walk Sienna to the bus stop every morning and be waiting for her in the evenings. It was nice and normal. We would go home every other weekend. It was good to see family. I was finally into the grove of things. Stefan was working two jobs and I was keeping the homestead afloat.

I wasn't totally alone in the city, my aunt Pearl lived about 20 minutes away. I would talk to her everyday and go see her some weekends. I loved her so much because she never judged us. The girls had my cousin Nic to help them adjust and to keep them company.

Our neighbors were getting on my last nerves! We stayed in a downstairs apartment. The neighbors upstairs had three kids. They would run and jump all day and most of the night. This went on for weeks. One day I had gotten tired of it. I got my coat walked upstairs, knocked on the door and waited for someone to answer. Finally a woman came to the door. I introduced myself after I greeted her and then I said, "Could you please ask the kids to stop jumping. It is very disturbing. I am trying to study". She apologized for the disturbance and said goodbye. Every other day I was up there asking her to keep the kids calm. I was in art school and they made it damn near impossible for me to study. Art has always been my passion and an escape for me. Art calms my nerves and gives me a piece of mind, something I needed to function.

Well we ended up moving to an upstairs apartment because our down stairs apartment flooded. Such a blessing in disguise. No more noisy neighbors! The upstairs apartment had a view. the downstairs apartment had a view of the woods it was on the back. It seems like the neighbors were nicer once we moved upstairs. They always spoke and their kids had manners.

Stefan had proven to be my rock, my strength, my lover, my friend and my soul mate. I am not going to pretend things were always peachy. Like all relationships you have your ups and downs. Fortunately our ups and down were minor. We could talk about everything. That was a good thing.

We ended up moving two more times, the first to another apartment complex across the street from the one we first lived in with Stefan and then we bought a house. I will start with the new apartment complex.

Ok this apartment was nice but the people were scary and doubtful. We managed. I walked the girls to the bus stop and waited for them in the evening. I met some of the neighbors, the Crosses. When the girls were in school

I would walk every morning. I noticed, after a few days of walking, there was this guy that would always be watching me. He wasn't nothing special and truth be told he gave me an uneasy feeling. It seemed like I had an admirer. Finally after a month of watching me, he approached me one day. I had the girls with me and we were walking back from my hair appointment (a lot of places were in walking distance) We spoke to be respectful. He stopped me and said, "*I like your hair*". I looked at him and said, "*thank you*". I started walking again. Again he stopped us. He was really getting on my nerves. He wanted to carry on a conversation and the girls and I just wanted to get home so we could eat lunch. Finally I blew him off and went home. Sade and Sienna both agreed he was strange and scary in a way. I had learned living at this apartment complex had its adventures. I was working. I was happy and my girls were happy. I ended up changing jobs (I was working through a temp service so the job didn't last long). My next job was actually fun I was answering the phone and taking reports on various complaints from the oil company. It was a ways out but it was a job. One day I was at work and the woman sitting next to me was just rude when she answered the phone. She was talking so loud that my customer could hear her through my phone. She was messy, weighed about three hundred pounds and was very unprofessional at all times. This particular day she was getting on my nerves. Every day it was the same thing with this woman. She was never polite on the phones at all. The thing that pissed me off the most was she found it hard to follow rules. We were not supposed to eat at our desk. This biddy had a huge jar of peanut butter on her desk eating eat with her fingers, talking on the phone and being rude. All of this she was doing loudly. One of my co-workers asked her to be a bit more quite she couldn't hear her customer. She went off on her. My client hung up because she couldn't hear and that pissed me off. I went to my supervisor and I said, "*Please do something with Martha! She has got to be the most arrogant, rudest and impolite,not to mention loud person I have ever seen! Do something about her or everybody over there will kick her ass. Believe me it will take everybody to beat her ass!*" My supervisor looked at me and said, "*Tee I didn't know you had all that spunk in you!*" I couldn't do nothing but laugh. I explained to him what the problem was. They kept an eye on her and listened in on all of our calls. Sure enough our customers were complaining of her being too loud. she was fired on the spot. this job was great. I worked on holidays and got the extra pay as well as some weekends. It soon came to an end.

Not long after I was working at a Bank processing loan applications. Never done the job before but it was easy to do. It was nice and a good experience. I met a lot of cool people and a lot of not-so-cool people. I had to catch about 4 buses and 4 trains to get to work. Yep I was up at 4am taking the girls to the babysitter and walking to the first bus stop which was about a half of mile from the apartments. One thing for sure is I got all the exercise I needed. I was so scared being out at dusk walking to the bus stop by myself. I kept pens in my pocket if I should need to defend myself. We had to dress the part for this job. I wore tennis shoes for the walking I had to do but then I would change when I got to work. If I came home late in the evenings Stefan and the girls would pick me up from the train station closest to our apartment. I was always early so I got a head start on some of the work. I explained to the supervisor I would be early a lot of mornings because I had to catch 4 buses and 4 trains to get here and if I didn't leave early I would get her about 30 minutes late. So they always left a note on my desk telling me what I needed to do. It was mostly filing. I didn't mind. The thing I didn't like about the job was riding the buses and trains and standing out in the heat or cold at the bus stops. I had so many ear infections, throat infections and more allergies than I needed or ever had known.

Now I belonged to a certain clique-not by choice. They seemed to have adopted me my first day. There was Charmane, a bi-sexual woman who was very opened about it, Tommy—a young husband who didn't really know the meaning of commitment, Adrienne-a older woman who looked like she was in her late twenties with a body of a teenager, and Janice—who was a single mom hung up on her baby's daddy and not to mention a drama queen. This was indeed a very colorful crew. We would go out to lunch together and just have fun. It took me a minute but I soon realized Charmane had her eyes on me. Charmane wasn't the only one who had their eyes on me. The guy in the mail room, Edgar also had his eyes on me. Edgar was about 6feet 5 inches and buffed (not my type). he dressed the part and he made himself look good. Adrienne wanted him so bad she had done damn near everything to get his attention. I picked Edgar to be a player, I was right. He was a player and a single parent. Give him his props on the parent part but that is about it. If it wasn't Charmane trying to get my attention it would be Edgar. One day Charmane and I were emailing each other. She said, "*here comes Edgar, he's coming your way*". I changed my screen quick. Edgar approached my desk and said, "*Ms Jones I need to see you in my office asap!*" I looked at Charmane with this clueless look. She shrugged her shoulders. I looked at Edgar and said, "*Sure give me a minute to finish this report*". He went to his office. I looked at Charmane and she had this grin on her face. I went over to her desk and said, *"what the hell?"* she said *"I don't know but tell me"*. I went to Edgar's office, I knocked on the door and he motioned me to come in. He looked me up and down and said, *"Tee you look nice today. You look nice every day. I just thought you should know that."* I am thinking to myself what the hell was that about. I looked at him and said, *"My man thinks I look nice everyday as well! Thank you, I do try."* he looks at me with this smirk on his face, walks up to me and says, *"you don't have to try you are the type of woman that just looks good, and you do look good!"* I excused myself and went back to my desk. Charmane quickly sent me an email, *"What he say?"* I wrote her back, *"He said I had it going on."* Charmane writes back, *"tell us something new we know you fine. you look like a glass of wine to me."* I wrote her, *"Thanks Charmane but you treading on thin ice"*. then I looked across to her at her desk walked over to her and said, *"Stop being fresh Charmane"*. She looked at me and laughed, *"Can't hurt to try Tee. You know we cool. Ain't no crossing the lines here."*

My job was fun and if I had to work weekends I could take the girls with me. The girls were amazed when I took them to the office. You see the decorating committee had the place decked out for Halloween. It was nice. I met lots of interesting people at the job but Adrienne and I were the closest and hung out the most. In the end I would miss that job. Well nothing last for long. My assignment along with my clique was over and we all went our separate ways. Adrienne and I stayed in touch. I didn't work for a long time after that. I stayed home with the girls and chilled. I was bored out of my mind. I went back to school.

Our Last Move

Well it was moving time again. Sienna was in the 3rd grade and Sade was in pre-K. Paying rent at an apartment was crazy. Once you think about it you realize you could have saved up enough money to buy two houses. We found a realtor and we started looking for houses. The day we found the house we wanted Sade was out of school because she wasn't feeling well. I thought it was a cold or something. We were looking at house and Sade was on my back. She had a hard time walking. I assumed her chest was congested. We had looked at so many homes. We had no intentions of looking at the house we would later call home. Sade shouted, *"stop let's look at this one"*. So we went into the house. It was nice. Stefan looked at me and said, *"Well?"* I said. *"this is it we don't need to look at any more"*. So we begin the process on making that house our home.

Sade seemed to be getting worse. Her breathing sounded funny. She kept telling us she couldn't breathe. I looked at her and I was concerned. Stefan totally misjudge that one. He thought nothing wasn't seriously wrong and we didn't need to take her to the emergency room. He was wrong. I called the ambulance, I was scared. The rescue unit for the fire station was the first ones there at the apartment. They asked me some questions and then they asked Sade some questions and they examined her. The firefighter looked at me and said, *"you called just in time she's having an asthma attack, a bad one."* Unbelievable we didn't even know she had asthma. They loaded Sade in the rescue unit and we were off to the children's hospital. She was admitted and I was a wreck. Later Stefan, Sienna, and the Crosses came to visit Sade. The Crosses stayed for a while said their goodbyes and left. Stefan sat on the bed with Sade and hugged her. He felt like he had let her down. Little did we know there would be a lot of future hospital visits and stays.

It was moving time. We had closed on the house and now it was time to pack up and move! Family came to help us move. It started off as a nice day, then came the storm. It was exciting because Stefan's family helped us to move and they were our first guests. Awesome. People were upstairs down stairs just everywhere. I was tickled and tired. Everything was un packed and put in its place. I was just thankful for the help. Family went home and it was just us. Sienna was in the third grade and once again Sade was home with me because they didn't offer the pre-K program. Our house was beginning to feel like a home.

It wasn't long before the school year had ended and a new one had beginned. Both girls were in school. Sienna was for some reason just not herself. I made so many trips to that school and had so many encounters with that crazy principal I was almost tired of seeing the place. Sienna was in fifth grade when Sade got sick. It was during the summer and my nephews were visiting. I was downstairs when I heard them yelling for me. I ran up the stairs to see what was wrong. My nephews were crying. I looked at them and, asked *"what's wrong?"* Sienna looked at me with tears in her eyes and they all said, *"Sade in the bathroom screaming. Something is hurting her real bad, we scared!"* I went to the bathroom door. I could hear Sade crying. *"Baby what's wrong?* she replied, *"it hurts!"* I asked her, *"are you doing number one or two?"* she replied between sniffles, *"number two"*. I then asked, *"hard or soft?"* she replied, *"soft"*. I asked, *"how soft?"* she replied, *"like water"*. Right away I ha reasons to be concerned. I really became concern when she came out the bathroom and I went in to look in the toilet, there was a lot of blood. Stefan and the kids looked at me waiting for an explanation. I looked at them and said, "we *need to get her to the Emergency room now!*" We spent 13 long hours at the emergency room just for them to tell us they haven't gotten a clue. Poor child was tested for everything you could think of including worms. Month after month Sade went from doctor to doctor and there were no answers. The child had lost so much weight that she looked different. She was frail. She was too weak to walk. She was barley eating. She had a colonoscopy and an endoscopy. I hated to see her go through so much. I felt helpless and the pain she was in, was making me tired and mad.

Finally A Diagnosis

Seeing Sade waking up after her surgery spooked me. My child looked dead just lying there motionless. My mom and her sister was there with us. I walked into the room and saw my baby looking dead and ran out. I told my aunt she could go in, I needed to call the school. The first phone call I made was to Sienna at her school. Everybody was relieved to hear she made it through the surgery without complications. I then called Sade's school and gave them the news. My next call would be to Stefan. Meanwhile Sade was waking up my aunt came out and I went back in. It was scary. She was woke but she was still feeling the effects of the meds. She had to wear a diaper because she wouldn't be alert enough to use the bathroom. The doctor still couldn't give us a diagnosis finally I knew what I had to do. I had to take her to the children's hospital in Atlanta. We drove two hours to have this procedure done and we would be going home with no answers to our questions. I was more frustrated than ever. I went to go get the car, and pulled it around to pick Sade up. My mom put her in the front seat and laid it back covered her with a blanket and she got in the back seat. My aunt was a basket case. She gave Sade a hug and we left to take mom home and hit the road. We dropped mom off and her co-worker came out and said, "*how the baby doing?*" I told him, "*as well as expected.*" He said, "*I know you need to get home but wait a few minutes tornado going towards that way. You don't want to be in that.*" We waited about 20 minutes and then we left. Sure enough the tornado had done some damage. We had to stop because of all the rain and the fallen trees. We were riding behind the tornado. I was scared. finally we made it home. I was tired. I blew the horn so Sienna could open the door. I had to carry Sade in the house and up the stairs to her room. Poor thing was out like a light. It took two full days for the meds to wear off and for her to be able to walk. She stayed out of school the rest of the week. Her classmates (all of third grade) had made her cards. they were so sweet.

Sade's illness affected everybody. Sienna was having issues at school just withdrawing from everyone and lashing out. Her teacher said she was always sad and crying. I had to explain about Sade and then it made a lot of sense to them. Everybody was on edge we still didn't know what was wrong with her.

I often thought I was being punished for something I had done. I was depressed. I had a child who use to be healthy and now she is so frail and sick for no apparent reason at all and I didn't think that was fair. This would prove to be a long journey for her and us. The thing that pissed me off the most was Sammy and his absences. I didn't care if he couldn't stand me at least act like you care when it comes to your child. Stefan had proven to be more than a father to those girls. He was there with them through everything the good and the bad.

No one knows the pain of having a terminally ill child. No one knows the stress it can have on that child as well as the family. The struggles were very hard.

I made Sade's appointment at the Children's Hospital. Finally we had a diagnosis. After numerous of tests and other surgical procedures we had a diagnosis. I was relieved. The first diagnosis was Lymphoma. One I wasn't willing to accept. The second one was Leukemia. I wasn't going to accept that either. Sade told the doctor's, "*If I should die tomorrow I will be a happy child because I lived a blessed life."* The doctors had tears in their eyes and so did I. We couldn't believe how strong this child was. The final diagnosis was H.E.S-Hyper Eosoniphilla Syndrome. Her cells that fight off infections were rapidly multiplying and attacking the body. They wasn't sure what the damage or the outcome would be. They did know it could be treated. It wasn't curable but it was treatable. This would be a long road of ups and downs. My child was strong and I was going to be just as strong for her. There were many hospital visits and stays. Everything that Sade had was chronic even her asthma, and that was the reason for her hospital visits (at least most of them). We went to appointment after appointment. We saw specialists after specialist and they became a part of our family. The doctors were just like family as well as their staff.

Sade was doing well in school although she had missed so many days she didn't fall behind in her work. The day came when we had another hurdle to jump. Sade was unable to walk, she was in a lot of pain. This was caused from nerve damage due to H.E.S. Three months she couldn't walk. She either used crutches or she was in a wheel chair. Her activities were no more. This was a challenge for us all. Sade had a good spirit about herself. Everyone expected her to just be sad and depressed. She was sad but she didn't let that get in her way. Kids teased her because she was in a wheel chair. It bothered her but she got passed it. It had been exactly three months, when Sade had decided she couldn't take it no more, she would walk again no matter how painful it was. I heard a crash, I ran to Sade's room. She had threw her crutches across the room. She was on the floor crying. *"I am tired of these crutches! I am tired of not being able to walk! I am tired of being picked on! I am sick and tired of being sick!"*

the next thing I knew Sade stood up and she fell. She was persistent she didn't want my help. She kept trying to walk on her on. Each time she fell she got right back up. three hours later she was walking through the hall saying *"Look I am walking and it hurts but it feel so good!"* Her physical therapy lasted about three or four months. It was tough but she didn't care all she wanted to do was walk. Walk is what she did.

We had good days and bad days. Sade entered a writing contest and wrote a story about her illness with her sister's help. She won for county. Here's her story:

It was a hot summer day when H.E.S rolled into town. H.E.S was no ordinary little fellow. In fact H.E.S wasn't little at all. He was twenty five letters long and lasted a life time. It took Teannaville by storm!

Teannaville was usually a happy, spirited, and carefree town. So this storm that rolled in with H.E.S started off **hard** and **strong**. The townspeople were in an uproar, they didn't know what to do. They called the mayor, Mrs. Mack. Mrs. Mack was as lost as a chicken with no head. First she called Mr. Triage to take the town's people temperature and vital signs. Thirteen hours had passed and Mayor Mack still didn't have a clue as to what H.E.S had done to the townspeople. Mayor Mack called her advisor Misra to shed some light on the situation. Misra invited his colleagues, Colonoscopy and Endoscopy. Colonoscopy and Endoscopy invited Relaxation and Knockout, just in case they needed back up.

Meanwhile the town's people were getting worse. Even Mayor Mack was clueless. Misra, Endoscopy, Colonoscopy, Relaxation, and Knockout were working hard to solve the mystery of the storm that had rolled in with H.E.S. The town was falling into a dreary state; it wasn't looking good for Teannaville at all. A terrible time had fallen on the town. No one knew what to do or how to do it.

Time passed and the town's people grew worse. Finally Mayor Mack decided to call some outsiders in to town to help her people. She called Mr. Runns, Iccey, Tenfoe Muhammad and Dee. It wasn't long before Runns went running away in a state of craziness. After a few days of deliberating and sorting through some things, Iccey and the crew decided to call in Biopsy, I.V., Faith, Emotion, and Hope. I.V was there to help with treatments, Biopsy was there to test the people, Faith was there for encouragement and support and Hope was there for love and inspiration. Four months had passed and H.E.S decided to make his presence known. He boldly attacked Mrs. Belly and caused Reflux to flare its ugly head. Night after night H.E.S and Reflux caused problems for the town's people and Mrs. Belly. Soon they were attacking the Testines. Their attack on Lunger failed as did their attack on Hearty. The town's people had gotten enough strength to fight back, it was a hard fight they knew they could not easily win but they tried with all their might. Teannaville had lost their strength after fighting H.E.S and Reflux but it was worth it. H.E.S and Reflux were slowing down and finding it hard to fight the town's people.

The war between H.E.S and the townspeople lasted a long time. In fact it is still going on. The townspeople are relying on the Aflac center to end this war.

I am a nine year old girl, living in Georgia. In December 2008 I was diagnosed with H.E.S.

Hyper Eosinophilia Syndrome is a rare blood disease that can cause problems for the body. My Eosinophilia cells (cells that fight bacteria and infections) are multiplying rapidly in my body and making me go through tough times. Some days are better than others. There is no cure for H.E.S. Like cancer it can go in to remission. I have recently started a steroid treatment, a very high dosage. I am on a low calorie diet and can no longer do any sports.

The one thing I refuse to do is to feel sorry for myself. I am alive, I am loved, I am happy, and I am here. I live for today, tomorrow, and for those who have lost hope. I will fight today and everyday to get better. The positive things that has come out of this is my sister is making necklaces, key chains, and bracelets and donating half of her proceeds to the Aflac Blood and Cancer Center. So if you should see one of my sister's key chains make sure you purchase one or two for a good cause. Keep me in your prayers; the power of prayer is awesome.

We were proud of Sade and so were the teachers. No matter how sick she is her spirit was always as bright as a ray of sunshine. Since she wrote her story her H.E. S has gone into remission. We haven't had a lot of problems with her asthma. Her regional Pain Syndrome affected her twice since she was diagnosed. The second time it only lasted for three weeks.

We are blessed and I no longer see it as a punishment. I see it as a road we as a family had to take to strengthen us and our bond. I say to all men and women, young and old the power of prayer is awesome and it works.

Getting through the Struggle & Moving On

Sade is a normal 11 year old and Sienna is a normal 16 year old. Struggles don't last long. Sammy keeps in touch with the girls. Kelly has moved and is doing fine. My family and I are on good terms. Stefan has been my back bone and my best friend through all of this. There came a time when I asked heavenly father to take the drama out of my life and fill it with positive energy. Sure enough people were dropped and others were put into my life for a positive reason.

Since I am starting my own business I felt the need to get rid of certain people that was around me because their karma wasn't positive. Art is still my passion and I paint. This is how I met aunt Al and Miss Dee.

My sister in-law, Mesa was telling me about a good friend of hers who may be able to give me some pointers on my business ventures. The first thing I thought was, maybe this person is into art. True this person was into art but on a totally different level. There was a lot Mesa wasn't telling me but it never crossed my mind. She was my sister in-law and would never steer me wrong. Mesa was the kind of woman that just attracted men of all kinds. She had a way with them that just cracked me up. That was my girl, true to the end no matter what. Mesa and her children would come and visit us whenever she had long weekends from work.

Mesa gave Aunt Al my number and we began talking from there. What really tripped me out was the first time

I spoke with her over the phone. I answered the phone, *"hello?" "Is this Ms Tee?" "yes it is". "This Aunt Al. I want you to stop holding back when it comes to making money. I see money all around you. You need to let them talents of yours flow so the money can rush right in."* I did exactly what she told me and before I knew it I was selling my paintings. this women was awesome and on the money.

The Rose That Was Left Behind

(Savon Christy, June 2011)

School after School, after school, after school. He came and he left, he came and he left and never returned again.

As he left he slowly hit the switch of life . . . .

as he took the sunshine that we needed to grow, the light we used to see at night and the energy we needed to keep going in life.

as each petal from the rose fell to the ground, petal by petal

second by second, minute by minute, hour by hour, day by day, week by week, month by month and then year by year.

When the gardener left the dying rose, the rose had a life of no food, water, light or energy. At this time friends came to the rescue. They helped the rose to rebuild life when family was harsh.

your friends gave you energy for three. As the leaves on the trees around you started to fall off

your petals came back petal by petal, your colored was restored.

You became an independent mother rose who could provide for her babies.

You have found the one rose who has completely restored and rebuilt your rose.

you are now a huge gorgeous rose, with color like a human's blood.

Even through the hurt and the darkness you found your way through.

I dedicate this poem to all the mothers who had to struggle to raise their kids because the fathers walked out and family was of no help. Especially my mom for seeing her way through all the hurt and bad my dad left behind. Most of all to the kids who had to watch their mother's struggle.

Introduction

Here is the same story you just heard about, the only difference is, it is written from my point of view. My name is Sienna and I love life. I am very sociable. When I was younger I went through a lot of hard times. I hope that people never take life for granted. The good can turn to bad anytime it wants too. Have you ever wondered what goes through a child's mind when someone they admire and love has crumbled their world? This story is for all who have wondered and those who have experienced it.

Losing Dad

I sat in my room all nervous and excited. My father was visiting. He had been away for many months. This would be my last time laying eyes on the father I admired and loved. His visits were never long. I sometimes wished he wouldn't come because when he left it broke my mom's heart. He always arrived with many stories and a whole lot of laughs.

I was so excited about my father coming for a visit. I was sure this would be the time he would pack up all our belongings and take us with him. That didn't and would never happen. I could hear my mother calling my name. Her voice was filled with excitement. My dad was driving up in the yard. I could see the excitement on my mom's face when she greeted my uncle Ralph and when she hugged my dad. The embrace was long and full of emotions.

She couldn't control the tears, and he had tears in his eye when he saw my mom, Sade and me. He went on and on about how he missed us and how he loved us. For a while I believed he loved us. Then it was time for him to leave. He was leaving without us! I wanted answers! I couldn't believe my father was leaving without us! My heart shattered into a million pieces, and a million more when I saw the tears streaming down my mother's face and the look of pain and fear in her eyes. This was the day my heart grew cold.

Each day I sat and watched my mom wait by the phone for my dad to call. It would be many days later when he finally called. Each time she would smile. Soon the smiles turned to tears. Without my mom having to say a word

I knew he would never come back. My mom turned to religion (not that she didn't believe in it before) She seemed to be happy. Looks were deceiving, she was still crying. Night after night I would lay next to my mom and Sade and listen to her cry. I just couldn't understand why he was doing this to her. My mom was crumbling like a cookie right in front of my eyes.

As minutes, hours, days, weeks, months and years passed by we as a family went through many hardships and heartaches. I started misbehaving in school thinking he would come back home if he knew I was sad. That didn't happen. Instead I made things harder for my mom. The burden that my mom had on her shoulders would have made the strongest of the strong turn weak. It only made my mom stronger.

After my dad walked out, it got . . . well stressful. He left no money, we had no water or electricity. This was very hard for us because my mom didn't have a job and no money at all. this is where I tell you how this affected me. First of all I was put on meds and labeled, all because I didn't know how to channel my anger. I felt like a zombie. The meds were horrible and they would start to wear off after five months. This is when the money hungry doctor decides to up the dosage (Now you knew the meds weren't working why up the dosage . . . just crazy). After a while I became very distant. Often my little cousin would be with me and my mom. He was like my brother and best friend. Even though I went to visit my aunt and my great grandfather to give my mom piece of mind, I could still tell she was very heart broken. At one point I thought she would just curl up and die. And then Sade and I would be lonely forever. One day out of nowhere it is like God blessed her with the strength to move and prove family wrong and make a great life for herself and for her kids. It was so hard for me because I was Daddy's little girl. never thought in a billion years he would leave me. I was so attached to him and he just ripped himself away like I didn't matter.

New School

As time goes on my school is rezoned. Which only meant one thing . . . new school. New school, new friends and being out of place. I left my friends, not that it was my choice to leave them behind. The new school was farther away which meant a longer bus ride. This was hard for me. I was so young and the kids were so mean. They often asked where my day was I lied and told them he was out of town. Technically he was out of town. they would often say I was lying and I didn't have a dad. I would look at them and try not to let the tears roll down. The only friend at the school, at first was Cheyenne and she ended up moving into our neighborhood. Every day after school and homework we played. I remember eating dinner with Cheyenne and her family one night. Cheyenne was in the shower when the lights went out. You could hear her screaming and crying for miles. Crying because she couldn't get out the bathroom and screaming because she couldn't see. funny I sort of felt like that when my dad left us.

I also remember a boy from the other school I used to go to. We were sort of in the same situation the only difference was . . . his mom walked out on him. This is when I noticed his Dad was into my mom. Who wouldn't be she looked like a teen ager not a mom. My mom doesn't age fast but I was almost sure she would after my dad up and left us. They were friends and nothing more only because my mom wanted it that way. He tried hard but it just didn't work. It wasn't long before I could see this entire situation was taking a toll on mom.

Bad Family

I always thought family was the best thing that could ever happen to a child. I thought they were supposed to love and cradle you and help you up when you were down. Well as far as I am concerned that family is only in fairy tales. I mean who in the freak could sit by and watch a young mom and her kids struggle and suffer? they not only watched us suffer but they also talked trash about us and some wouldn't even help us. they weren't perfect! Who were they to judge my mom! It just wasn't fair! My aunt called child services on my mom. Why? Because she was trying to support her kids or was it because our neighbors were helping us out? my mom was broken into tiny pieces and I couldn't stand seeing her like this. This is what some family members want to see her down so they could kick her farther down. It wasn't right! Mom did everything she could to make things right for us, everything legally possible. I couldn't believe the enjoyment they were getting out of seeing their own flesh and blood suffer. Whenever my aunt came for a visit so did trouble. We ended up living in this home for people with problems for three months, and that was all my aunt's fault. I hated it. It still makes me mad when I think of the time spent at that place.

I did not want my baby sister living a life like this. Night after night I prayed for a miracle. Day after day I hoped for a change. It broke my mom's heart. She was barely holding on to sanity and this worried me. So what if she always had a smile on her face. I knew my mom and I knew her world was falling apart. When my mom's friend came to get us it was like breaking out of jail. I don't know what made my mom call her but it should have made her do it sooner. When her friend heard where we were she was pissed. She was calling my dad a weak ass man and a good for nothing for putting us through this shit. I couldn't disagree with her at all. Family can be good but they can also degrade you, put you in the dirt and drag you down when you are up. funny how family says they are here to help . . . where was the help when we needed it. they were all talk and no help. they tried to ruin my mom's life and got made when she gained control of her life.

Moving in with Miss Kim
& Meeting Stefan

After taking control of her life again my mom was offered a job. She needed a babysitter and a house cleaner. My mom really had no clue what she had gotten into until she saw the house. It was a mess! Her son and I were the same age and her youngest daughter was Sade's age. It took my mom forever to clean that place it was yucky! I would not have cleaned it with five pairs of gloves. Well at least we had a roof over our heads and my mom had money in her pockets.

It wasn't so bad living there. What I couldn't understand is why she needed a house cleaner and a baby sitter when her parents lived with her. They looked like they were able to watch the kids and clean. Oh well maybe it was one of them grown up things I knew nothing about. We had some good times with them and they became family.

My mom ended meeting Kim's brother Stefan. He was nice. Just like my mom he could pass for a teenager. I liked him he seemed to be good people, but it was my duty to give him a hard time. That is just what I did, gave him a hard time. I thought if I acted all hard he wouldn't want to be around. Once again I was wrong! He helped us pack up the old house and move to another one. My mom's friend (more like my dad's friend who was pissed at him for leaving us like trash) gave my mom a job and the job came with an apartment on the property. Yep My mom had a new job title; Leasing Agent/Property Manager. She was happy so I had no complaints.

Now Stefan seemed to be around more and more. He stayed three hours away and found the time to spend with me, Sade and mom. I could tell my mom was into him. It was this look she had in her eyes-strange and in a kid's mind just yucky. We stayed in this place about seven months and things were good. I eventually stopped being a hassle and a handful.

Stefan

Then one day the strangest thing happened-Stefan asked my mom if we would move in with him. Now I don't know what my mom was thinking but I was like—What! Well we sold a bunch of our things (mom says it is better to have money than two of everything) packed up the rest and moved to the city. I could see it was hard on my mom and I at first. It was strange but I can adapt to any situation and that is just what I did. My mom had some cool jobs. She worked through a temp service so nothing was long, but she made good money. We moved a total of three times. The last move was just that the last move. We moved into our very own house and it was nice we had a yard and a big back porch. Family helped us move, we had fun although it stormed really bad.

We had been in the house a while before Sade got sick. It made no sense at all, one day she was fine and the next day she was very sick. I was scared. This wasn't a minor sick like a bug or something this was a serious sick. Two years I watched my mom act like she was so brave. Sade was very sick. Somebody had to have a strong back bone. My mom never cried in front of Sade, she never wanted to worry her. I knew better. Her nor Stefan could hide their fear from me. I was a wreck. I cried at school I fought at school, I just had no place to put the anger that I was feeling. I was mad. I was mad at Yahweh for allowing my sister to be sick. I was mad at myself for being mean to her sometimes. I was mad at my dad for not caring. I was mad. We went through some hard times. Sade's appointments would drain her sometimes.

All the painful procedures she had to go through before they found out what was wrong with her hurt me to my soul. T see someone you love struggle and not look familiar to you was damn near devastating. I loved my sister and I didn't want to give her up not now or ever! My sister didn't complain about being sick. She was strong. It was a long journey but we got through it as a family. Sade wrote this wonderful story about her illness with my help. She won for county. We were proud of her. No matter how sick she was, her education never suffered. She stayed on the honor roll, although she missed a lot of days.

Stefan changed our lives. Yahweh thought we deserved to have one of his angels and we are so thankful for him. True we had our ups and downs but we got through the best way we knew how as a family. My mom is all the way overboard in love with him. He is our father our life line our friend and he is strict. I have to say we are doing well. I am older and wiser. I use to blame my mom for my dad leaving. now I know It wasn't my place to judge and it wasn't her fault. We are blessed and being blessed feels so good to me.

The End

Acknowledgements

First I would like to thank Heavenly Father Yahweh for all of his love power and strength. Without him none of this would have been possible.

I would like to thank my Stefan for giving me the courage to write this book and for having my back through it all. Without his love, understanding and admiration I don't think it would have been an easy task.

I would like to thank my children for never ever giving up through the struggles. I would like to thank my sister in law for giving me some useful insights on life as well as aunt Al. My family is the ones who gave me something to write about and I thank them for that.

I would Like to thank Miss Alanna for the use of her poem and Miss Te'Anna for the use of her story.

I would like to think the Kelly in my life. We have been through some good and bad times and she was a friend from start to finish.